REVIVAL 101

UNDERSTANDING HOW CHRIST IGNITES HIS CHURCH

BY DALE SCHLAFER

NAVPRESS®

A *Pray!*® Magazine Book

Pray! Books • P.O. Box 35004 • Colorado Springs, CO 80935
www.praymag.com

Dedication

To, and for, "the one who loves me and gave His life for me,"
my blessed Lord Jesus Christ.

And to the one who loves me and gives herself up for me,
especially in intercessory prayer, my wife, Liz.

Contents

Preface

Today, revival seems to be on the lips of Christians everywhere! Ten years ago, few were speaking about it at all. But in the last decade, revival praying and the amount of literature on revival have grown tremendously. And we have seen both true and false revival occur in small, isolated cases across America. These reports are awakening the church to the issue of revival.

However, during this same time frame, I have observed that many Christians are uninformed about the subject of both personal and corporate revival. Burdened by this realization, the need for a revival stimulus became the focus of my prayer and eventually gave birth to the idea of a primer (a basic instructional guide) about revival. The purpose of *Revival 101* is to stimulate your interest in revival. I want you to become convinced of the desperate need of the church for a fresh encounter with the Lord Jesus Christ. It is my passionate desire that when you finish this book, you will determine to pursue your relationship with the Lord Jesus Christ with greater fervor. It is also my prayer that you will pursue further this subject of revival and awakening. To that end, there are many good books on revival listed at the back of this book.

While in no way is this meant to be an exhaustive, scholarly work on revival, it is my prayer that the Author of all revival, our precious heavenly Father, might be pleased to use this primer to spur you on to an interest in and a passionate desire for both individual and corporate revival.

Before you start reading, I challenge you to pray this prayer: "Father, I ask You to open the eyes of my heart so as I read, I might have heavenly insight and discernment to discover Your heart concerning revival."

CHAPTER ONE

What Is Revival?

On February 3, 1970, students and faculty members at Asbury College in Wilmore, Kentucky, walked into Hughes Auditorium for what they assumed would be a routine chapel. Students at this Christian liberal arts college were expected to attend chapel three times each week. But it proved to be anything but routine!

On that Tuesday morning, Custer Reynolds, Asbury's academic dean and a Methodist layman, was in charge. Instead of preaching, Reynolds briefly gave his testimony. He then issued an invitation for students to talk about their own Christian experiences. There was nothing particularly unusual about that.

One student responded to his offer. Then another. Then another. Then, without warning, heaven broke loose. Students started pouring to the altar. A dam of pride broke under the presence of God.

Many came weeping to the front to kneel in repentance, others gave testimonies including confession of sin. All this was mixed with spontaneous singing. Lectures were cancelled for the day as the auditorium filled with more than 1,000 people. Few left for meals. By midnight more than 500 still remained praying and worshiping. Hundreds committed their lives to Christ that day. By 6 a.m. the next morning (Wednesday), 75 students were still praying in the hall. Through the day the chapel filled as again all lectures were cancelled. The time was filled with praying, singing, confessions, and testimonies. Students and faculty sought out others whom they had wronged and asked for forgiveness.

Asbury, like many evangelical organizations, held annual, scheduled, so-called "revivals" with guest ministers and services booked in advance. This, however, was not the same. No one had planned it. And no one person was leading it.

News of the outpouring spread in newspapers and on television around the country. Strangers flocked to Wilmore to worship with the students. On Thursday, Asbury officials again dismissed classes. By Thursday, the presence of God had broken out at the seminary, across the street from the college.

What was supposed to have been a routine, 50-minute chapel service, instead lasted 185 hours nonstop. Intermittently, it continued for weeks. Ultimately, it spread across the United States and into foreign countries.

Something for Believers

What comes to mind when you hear the word *revival?* Although many are hearing the term revival these days, there is a lack of clarity as to its real meaning. For some of us, the word calls to mind a series of meetings held every year at church, usually focusing on trying to save the lost.

However, Scripture reveals that revival happens to *believers*, not the lost. A friend of mine notes, "You have to be 'vived' before you can be re-vived." He is right. The word *revival* speaks to Christians. And church history complicates the situation. Often the word *awakening* was used interchangeably with the word *revival.* For example, "The Great Awakening" is a term that speaks of both the revival of the church and the conversion of the lost. How do we bring clarity to this confusion?

In recent years, many have used the word *revival* to describe the work of God among those already saved and the word *awakening* to describe the lost coming to Christ. For the purpose of this book, the word *revival* refers to a sovereign work of God in the church among His people. The word *awakening* means a sovereign move of God among those both in and outside of the church who do not know Jesus Christ. Today, a uniformity regarding the use of the words *revival* and *awakening* is occurring in the church. Confusion is diminishing, as the above definitions are gaining acceptance.

But if revival is not a tent meeting, what is it? Others have described revival this way:

That strange and sovereign work of God in which He visits His own people, restoring, reanimating, and releasing them into the fullness of His blessings. (Stephen Olford)

The renewal of the first love of Christians, resulting in the awakening and conversion of sinners . . . It reclaims the backslidden church and awakens all classes. (Charles Finney)

Breathing the breath of God. (Robert Coleman)

Revival is God purifying His church. (Erwin Lutzer)

Revival is a people saturated with God. (Duncan Campbell)

The inrush of the Spirit into a body that threatens to become a corpse. (D. M. Patton)

A work of God's Spirit among His own people . . . what we call revival is simply New Testament Christianity, the saints getting back to normal. (Vance Havner)

Richard Owen Roberts, one of the leading figures in the revival movement of our day, has said that he now has come to the conviction that the best definition of revival is one word: GOD.

There is a very precious sense in which revival is literally God in the midst of His people. His manifest presence produces all that is desirable in revival. The absence of His manifest presence accounts for all that is undesirable during seasons of moral and spiritual decline that precede revivals. (Richard Owen Roberts)

Martyn Lloyd-Jones describes revival this way:

The essence of revival is that the Holy Spirit comes down upon a number of people together, upon a whole church, upon a number of churches, on districts, or perhaps a whole country. It is, if you will, a visitation of the Holy Spirit.

The Puritans were fond of speaking of the "manifest presence of God." By that, they meant

. . . those special times when God reveals His Son to a generation of His people in such a dramatic fashion that it seems to the Christian that Christ had been hidden from them, then suddenly made manifest. It is such a manifest working of God that human personalities are overshadowed and human programs abandoned. It is man retiring into the background because God has taken the field. It is the Lord . . . working in extraordinary power on the saint and sinner. (Arthur Wallis, *In the Day of Thy Power*)

This is the outstanding feature of revival: Suddenly, without warning, God is present and people are brought face to face with God's holiness and their sin. It seems that God is dealing with them alone so that whatever the spiritual state of the person, saved or unsaved, a mighty work of transformation occurs. The unsaved are brought to salvation (awakening), and the saved are brought to further holiness (revival).

But "preeminently, all true revival is about God bringing glory back to His Son by the power of the Holy Spirit through His church. . . . Yes, biblical revival is supremely Son-centered—it is utterly Christ dominated. . . . We can only think rightly about revival when we think rightly about Christ's place in revival" (*An Urgent Appeal*, p. 19*)*.

These definitions have a common thread running through them: God among people. He brings revival and renewal to the saved, He brings salvation to the lost, and He restores a love and passion for Jesus Christ.

QUESTIONS FOR REFLECTION

1. In your circle of Christian friends, is the term revival understood? Why or why not?
2. Which of the definitions given for revival resonates best with you? Why?
3. What elements of the experience at Asbury fit with these definitions of revival?
4. Do you agree or disagree with the statement that "we can only think rightly about revival when we think rightly about Christ's place in revival?" Why or why not?
5. In your own words define revival and awakening.

CHAPTER TWO

Is Revival Biblical?

It started with a longing. In the 1830s, Rev. Andrew Murray Sr. (the father of well-known pastor and author Andrew Murray) wanted to see revival come to South Africa. Murray devoted every Friday evening to prayer for revival. Later other similarly burdened ministers united with him in prayer. They prayed consistently for 30 years and waited in faith.

In Worcester, South Africa, Andrew Murray Jr.'s pastorate, God raised up a group of revival intercessors to pray for the people. They regularly prayed on a hilltop overlooking the village. The minister who preceded Murray intensely prayed and worked for revival.

In 1860, almost 30 years since the beginning of this prayer effort, God began to move. There had been a small church prayer meeting (three or four people) for months, but suddenly, almost overnight, young and old, parents and children, without distinction of color, flocked to that prayer meeting, driven by a common impulse to cast themselves before God and utter their cries of repentance. In places where prayer meetings were unknown a year before, the people now complained because meetings ended an hour too soon! Not only weekly but daily prayer meetings were demanded by the people, even three times a day—and even among children.

This quote from an eyewitness, Rev. J. C. deVries, gives us a clearer picture of what happened at Worcester (quotes taken from "Out of the Box," by Leona Choy, *Pray!*, Issue 22):

On a certain Sunday evening there were gathered in a little hall some sixty young people. I was leader of the meeting, which began with a hymn and a lesson from God's Word, after which I prayed. Three or four others gave out a verse of a hymn and prayed, as was the custom. Then a colored girl of about 15 years of age, in service with a nearby farmer, rose at the back of the hall and asked if she too might propose a hymn. At first I hesitated, not knowing what the meeting would think, but better thoughts prevailed, and I replied, "Yes." She gave out her hymn-verse and prayed in moving tones.

While she was praying, we heard, as it were, a sound in the distance, which came nearer and nearer, until the hall seemed to be shaken; with one or two exceptions, the whole meeting began to pray, the majority in audible voice, but some in whispers. Nevertheless, the noise made by the concourse was deafening.

A feeling which I cannot describe took possession of me. Even now, 43 years after these occurrences, the events of that never-to-be-forgotten night pass before my mind's eye like a soul-stirring panorama. I feel again as I then felt, and I cannot refrain from pushing my chair backwards, and thanking the Lord fervently for His mighty deeds.

While that meeting was going on, it seems that Murray was preaching in English elsewhere in the church building. He was not present during the beginning of the events. When his service was over, an elder passing the door of the hall heard the noise, peeped in, and ran to call Murray who returned with him at a run. The eyewitness continues:

Mr. Murray came forward to the table where I knelt praying, touched me, and made me understand that he wanted me to rise. He then asked me what had happened. I related everything to him. Then he walked down the room for some distance and called out as loudly as he could, "People, silence!" But the praying continued. In the meantime, I kneeled down again. It seemed to me that if the Lord was coming to bless us, I should not be upon my feet but on my knees.

Mr. Murray then called loudly again, "People, I am your minister sent from God! Silence!" But there was no stopping the noise. No one heard him, but all continued praying and calling on God for mercy and pardon.

Mr. Murray then returned to me and told me to start the

hymn-verse commencing "Help de ziel die raadloos shreit" (Aid the soul that helpless cries). I did so. But the emotions were not quieted, and the meeting went right on praying. Mr. Murray then prepared to depart, saying, "God is a God of order, and here everything is confusion!" With that he left the hall.

We may wonder why Murray, who had prayed fervently for revival, who had grown up praying for revival, would try to stop this move of God. (He soon realized it was of God and embraced it.) Some believers are quick to embrace anything supernatural as being from God. But Satan can mimic moves of God, so true believers should be cautious of unusual manifestations. But that does not mean we should out of hand reject them.

We should always ask this question regarding any subject: "Does the Word of God, the Bible, authorize its practice or belief?" In the case of revival, the word appears in its various forms more than 250 times in the Old Testament and five times in the New Testament. In both the Old and New Testaments, we find God reaching out continually, calling His followers to return to an intimate love relationship with Him.

Henry Blackaby's work on revival and awakening, entitled *Fresh Encounter*, discloses a cyclical pattern to the revivals of the Bible and church history.

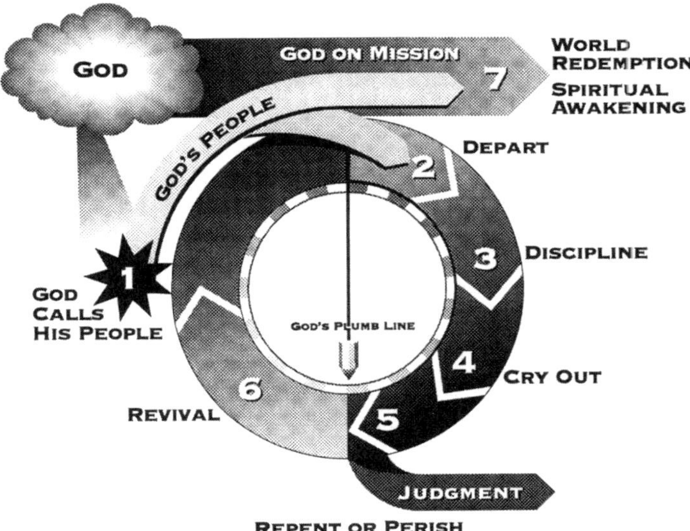

From *Fresh Encounter: God's Pattern for Revival and Spiritual Awakening.* © 1993 LifeWay Press. Henry T. Blackaby and Claude V. King, authors. Used by permission. All rights reserved.

This pattern can be seen in seven stages:

Phase 1: God is on a mission to redeem a lost world. He calls His people into relationship with Himself, and He accomplishes His work through them.

Phase 2: God's people depart from Him, turning to substitutes for His presence, purpose, and ways.

Phase 3: God disciplines His people out of His love for them that they would return to Him.

Phase 4: God's people cry out to Him for help.

Phase 5: God calls His people to repent and return to Him or perish.

Phase 6: God revives His repentant people by restoring them to a right relationship with Himself.

Phase 7: God exalts His Son Jesus in His people and draws the lost to a saving faith in Him.

Where do you see the church of America in the above cycle? As an individual, where are you? As I travel the country, I am encouraged. I believe we are somewhere between phases 4 and 5. We are almost at the critical point. Will we repent and return to Him? If we will, then revival cannot be far away. If we refuse, then further, more powerful judgment awaits.

How Long Do True Revivals Last?

Because of the cyclical nature of revival, it usually lasts only for a season. Some revivals are brief, while others last almost a generation. In either case, revival is not permanent. Hopefully, the "afterglow" for many people and churches changes them for years, and in some instances, for generations.

The following lists the outstanding revivals in the Old and New Testament that demonstrate the cyclical pattern of revival:

- **Jacob's household** — Gen. 35:1-15
- **Asa** — 2 Chron. 15:1-15
- **Joash** — 2 Kings 11-12; 2 Chronicles 23-24
- **Hezekiah** — 2 K. 18:4-7; 2 Chronicles 29-31
- **Josiah** — 2 Kings 22-23
- **Zerubbabel** — Ezra 5-6
- **Nehemiah** — Nehemiah 9-12

In both the Old and New Testaments, people departed from God, then responded to His call to return. In Revelation 2-3, we see the church, barely 50 years old, has already departed from a close relationship with God. The Lord calls the church to repent and return to an intimate love relationship (Rev. 2:2-4,14-16; 3:1,3,15-16,19).

The church has departed repeatedly throughout history from its close intimate relationship with God. As a result, it stands in need of a special work of God to reestablish this love relationship. It is beyond the scope of this book to deal with all the revivals in biblical and church history. If you wish to study this more in depth on your own, numerous works are listed in Appendix C.

One work particularly worth mentioning is *Historical Collections of Accounts of Revival*, by John Gillies, which documents revivals from the Bible through the end of the 18th century. This work shows that God has continued to revive His church throughout history because His people have continued the cycle of departure from Him.

QUESTIONS FOR REFLECTION

1. What reasons can you give as to why there are cycles of revival and awakening?
2. Where in the seven stages of the cycle of revival do you think the western church is? Why did you choose this cycle? Where would you place the church that you attend? Why?
3. Take some time to study the various biblical revivals mentioned to discover what led the people to depart from the Lord. Then examine yourself and the church you attend to see if any of these indicators are present.

CHAPTER THREE

Is There a Need for Revival in the Church Today?

The Hebrides Islands off the northwest coast of Scotland can be a cold place. In 1949, it was also a spiritually cold place. Not a single young person attended Sunday services. Many churchgoers were Christian in name only. Their lives were spiritually barren. The islands were quickly becoming a spiritual wasteland.

In October, 1949, the Free Church Presbytery on Lewis Island, the largest of the islands in the Hebrides, was troubled over the spiritual deadness of the church. There were few conversions. The Presbytery passed a resolution calling upon their faithful members to pray because of the devastated condition of the church.

Two elderly sisters, Peggy and Christine Smith, became burdened by the Holy Spirit to cry out for the souls of the Hebrides. In a small cottage in the village of Barvas, these two intensely sought the Lord. Because Peggy was blind and her sister was almost bent double with arthritis, both were unable to attend public worship. Their humble cottage became a sanctuary where they met with God.

After many nights of seeking the Lord, the two were persuaded of an impending move of the Holy Spirit. The sisters sent for the minister, the Rev. James Murray MacKay, and told him what God had shown them, asking him to call his elders and deacons together for special times of waiting upon God.

Three nights a week the leaders prayed together for many more months. One night, having begun to pray at 10 p.m., a young deacon read from Psalm 24 and challenged everyone to be clean before God. The young man cried out, "Oh God, are my hands clean? Is my heart pure?" He got no further, but fell prostrate to the floor, weeping under the weight of truth. An awareness of God filled the barn and a stream of supernatural power was let loose in their lives.

Shortly after that night, MacKay invited Duncan Campbell to come and lead meetings. At the close of his first meeting in the Presbyterian church in Barvas, the travel weary preacher was invited to join an all-night prayer meeting! Thirty people gathered for prayer in a nearby cottage.

When Campbell and his friends arrived at the church the next morning, the church was *already* crowded in anticipation of the night's meeting. People had gathered from all over the island. Large numbers were converted as God's Spirit convicted multitudes of sin. Many lay prostrate on the floor of the church, weeping. At the end of the day, Campbell attempted to pronounce the benediction, but a young man began to cry aloud to the Lord. He wept aloud and prayed for 45 minutes. The presence of the Lord rested upon the large crowd as weeping and worship filled the building. The crowds continued, with thousands outside worshiping and weeping before the Lord. The service continued until 4 a.m.

The Holy Spirit began to invade nearby towns, and the other islands as well. Nearly all the bars were completely shut down for lack of business. Young people came in droves to the churches as parents repented for not putting the Lord first in their hearts.

Churches all across the islands were packed as the heavenlies over the Hebrides were altered. The revival continued strongly through 1952 and had lasting impact for the next 30 years as the gospel and God's presence changed the lives of countless tens of thousands.

What Is Our Condition?

A quick look at American society today reveals that something is desperately wrong. Questions arise such as, "How do we account for the condition of our society? How did America end up as it is today?" The primary answer is this: The condition of America is due largely to the condition of the church.

Henry Blackaby says, "If society as a whole seems to be getting darker and darker, it is not the problem of the darkness: the darkness is just acting like its nature. But it is that the light no longer dispels the darkness, and the salt no longer preserves. It is time for the light to say, 'if things are darker, the problem is with us'" (*Foundation of Revival*, p. 72).

The following statistics and facts, gleaned in 2002, are taken from the findings of research groups, denominational publications, and books, illustrating the church's desperate condition and need for revival.

- In proportion to the U.S. population, there are less than half as many churches today as there were in 1900. Since 1950, there are 30 percent *fewer* churches for today's population.
- Roughly 4,000 churches are begun every year, while 7,000 die and close their doors.
- North America and Europe are the only continents in the world where Christianity is not growing.
- In 1991, 21 percent of all adults were unchurched. In 2002, 34 percent fit that description.
- The United States is the fourth largest unchurched nation in the world.
- Giving per person in the church is less today than it was during the Great Depression.
- The United States is the number two missionary-receiving country in the world, behind Brazil. This is how our brothers and sisters around the world view our commitment to Jesus Christ and the spiritual health of the American church.
- Researchers have discovered that 3,500 people leave the church every day in the United States.
- According to studies by the Association of Church Missions Committees, 250,000 of the 300,000 U.S. Protestant congregations are either stagnant or dying.
- In his book, *Death of the Church*, Mike Regele says: "Based on demographics alone, the future of the church is grim." Catholic, Protestant, Evangelical, and mainline churches all face the crisis of dwindling numbers.
- Born-again believers are more likely to experience a divorce than are non-born-again adults (27 percent vs. 24 percent).
- The average number of adults attending services of a Protestant church is 90. This reflects a 10 percent decline from 1997 and a 12 percent decline from 1992.

Let's be very clear: The institution is simply a reflection of the sum of the individuals. A denomination or fellowship is simply the sum total of all the churches in that group.

The church of Jesus Christ in America is in desperate need of revival. It is the belief of many today that if God does not bring revival soon, then like ancient Israel, nothing but a more intense judgment awaits us.

How did the church in America come to such a pathetic state? It has experienced a slow, incipient decline of belief and practice. It is like the familiar story of the frog and the kettle of water. If you place a frog in boiling water, it will jump out immediately because it can tell it is in a hostile environment. But if you place a frog in a kettle of room temperature water, it will stay there, content with its surroundings. As the temperature of the water slowly increases, the frog does not leap out, but just stays there, unaware that the environment is changing. If you continue to turn up the heat until the water boils, the frog will die content, unaware of the impending disaster it was facing. That is what has happened to the church. One pastor explained it this way:

> It is latent and hidden . . . The painful process of spiritual disease may be advanced in the soul so secretly, so silently, and so unobservedly, that the subject (the Christian man, woman, or young person) of it may have lost ground, may have parted with many graces and much vigor, and may have been beguiled into an alarming state of spiritual barrenness and decay, before even a suspicion of his real condition has been awakened in his breast. (Octavius Winslow, *Personal Declension*, pp. 101-102)

Many of us are like Samson after Delilah cut his hair: "But he did not know that the LORD had left him" (Jdg. 16:20). The church is filled with people like this, who are ignorant that the world, the flesh, and the devil have left them unaware that the manifest presence of God has left them.

Most of us are desensitized to the fact that we have stopped living with passion for our God. We are blinded to the fact that there is little about our life that now reflects a vital love relationship with Jesus Christ. The Bible calls this condition backsliding. "A backslider," says Richard Owen Roberts, "is a person who was once emptied of their own ways, and filled with the ways of God, but gradually allowed their own ways to seep back until they are all but empty of God and full of themselves again" (Roberts, *Revival,* p. 30).

Backsliding is the sin of crowding God out by filling one's life with self. Proverbs 14:14 says, "The backslider in heart will be filled with his own ways" (NKJV).

Are we a backslidden church? Are you backslidden? The following list by Roberts may be a good litmus test.

1. When prayer ceases to be a vital part of a professing Christian's life.
2. When the quest for biblical truth ceases and one grows content with the knowledge of eternal things already acquired.
3. When biblical knowledge possessed or acquired is treated as external fact and not applied inwardly.
4. When earnest thoughts about eternal things cease to be regular and gripping.
5. When services of the church lose their delights.
6. When pointed spiritual discussions are an embarrassment.
7. When sports, recreation, and entertainment are a large and necessary part of your lifestyle.
8. When sins of the body and of the mind can be indulged without an uproar in your conscience.
9. When aspirations for Christlike holiness cease to be dominant in your life and thinking.
10. When the acquisition of money and goods becomes a dominant part of your thinking.
11. When you can mouth religious songs and words without heart.
12. When you can hear the Lord's name taken in vain, spiritual concerns mocked, and eternal issues flippantly treated and not be moved to indignation and action.
13. When you can watch degrading movies and television and read morally debilitating literature without a prick of conscience.
14. When breaches of peace in the brotherhood are of no concern to you.
15. When the slightest excuse seems sufficient to keep you from spiritual duty and opportunity.
16. When you become content with your lack of spiritual power and no longer seek repeated endowments of power from on high.

17. When you pardon your own sin and sloth by saying the Lord
    understands and remembers that we are dust.
18. When there is no music in your soul and no song in your
    heart.
19. When you adjust happily to the world's lifestyle.
20. When injustice and human misery exist around you, and you
    do little or nothing to relieve the suffering.
21. When your church has fallen into spiritual declension and
    the Word of God is no longer preached there with power,
    and you are still content.
22. When the spiritual condition of the world declines around
    you and you cannot perceive it.
23. When you are willing to cheat your employer.
24. When you find yourself rich in grace and mercy and marvel
    at your own godlikeness.
25. When your tears are dried up and the hard, cold spiritual facts
    of your existence cannot unleash them. (Roberts, pp. 33-44)

With the psalmist, we pray:

Return to us, O God Almighty! Look down from heaven and
see! Watch over this vine, the root your right hand has planted,
the son you have raised up for yourself. Your vine is cut down, it
is burned with fire; at your rebuke your people perish. . . . Revive
us and we will call on your name. Restore us, O LORD God
Almighty; make your face shine upon us, that we may be saved.
(Ps. 80:14-19)

As we lament the condition of the church today, search the
Scriptures, and study revival history and the prayers of God's people,
it seems that there has never been a time in the history of the church
of Jesus Christ in America when revival and awakening was needed
more than our day.

1. What do you think about the last paragraph of this chapter? Do you agree with the author or disagree? Why?
2. What do you think has caused the church in the United States to come to its present state?
3. In the list regarding backsliding, how do you see yourself, your family, your church and/or ministry?
4. Are there other evidences in your church that it may have lost its passion for Jesus? List them.

CHAPTER FOUR

How Does Revival Come?

Iwas raised in a mainline denomination. As an adult, I began to attend a church that emphasized the priesthood of believers. Its focus was on worship. We learned psalms and spiritual choruses, and we began each service by standing and ministering in worship as a priest unto the Lord.

Something happened to this church. I can't say exactly when it began or ended, but it was ushered in through worship. The church experienced a visitation—an outpouring of the Holy Spirit—and we found ourselves engulfed in the presence of God.

During this time, God would come into our midst as we worshiped. The service would be taken out of the hands of the leader, and the Holy Spirit would begin to preside. We were brought to our feet spontaneously. Time had no meaning. Worship was joy, and we wanted to continue forever, expressing adoration, experiencing the Lord's presence and His glory. Revival had come to our church. (Dr. Corinthia Boone, *Pray!* Issue 4, p. 18)

What Can We Do?

By this time you may be sensing an ever-growing longing for revival—not only in your own heart, but in your church as well. But the question lingers: How does revival come? Can we do something to usher it in? The answer is no . . . and yes.

Revival originates in God's heart and rests in His sovereignty.

Basically, it comes when God is ready to send it. Tom Phillips says, "Revival springs from God's initiation, not from our determination. Revival is the new light and the life of God that comes in His time, for His purposes, to lead us out of wandering and back to Himself" (*Revival Signs,* p. 118).

The Bible warns us against thinking that it is something that we accomplish, through our efforts (Psalm 85; Is. 63:15-17; Isaiah 64; Zech. 4:6; Jn. 3:8; Acts 2:7,12). In the final analysis, human beings cannot predict its timing, precipitate its unfolding, or preclude its appearance. But, while we acknowledge God's sovereign work in revival, it is important that we not use this truth as an excuse to do nothing. God can and does use secondary means. Often He chooses to work in grace through our prayers, Bible studies, worship, fellowship, sacraments, and daily obedience. Like Jesus, we want to do what we see the Father doing (Jn. 5:19). When the Spirit of God moves us to certain actions as a precursor for revival, we must obey. Although our action does not bring the revival, if we do not do those things He has commanded, it is doubtful we will ever see revival.

"For it is God who works in you *to will* and *to act* according to his good purpose" (Phil. 2:13, emphasis added). In other words, even when we do certain activities, it is as a consequence of God's activity in our lives.

What Is the Spiritual Preparation for Revival and Awakening?

Prayer and Fasting

The first and most important preparation is *prayer* and *fasting.* Original accounts of revival and awakening almost universally include these two disciplines. In our own day, a tremendous movement exists to recapture these vital spiritual disciplines in the church in America.

Early American pastor Jonathan Edwards led a prayer effort that God used to bring The First Great Awakening (1734-1750). Edwards' interest in revival was sparked by a copy of a treatise on united prayer for revival that had come from Scotland. This so stirred him that he expanded it and wrote his own work entitled, in typical Puritan style, "An Humble Attempt to Promote Explicit Agreement and Visible Union of God's People, in Extraordinary Prayer, for the Revival of Religion and the Advancement of Christ's Kingdom on Earth." This was Edwards' call to Christians, and entire churches everywhere, to unite in a workable strategy of synchronized prayer. This strategy became known as a "concert of prayer." Edwards expected this idea to spread quickly to the church of New England because all Christians, regardless of denomination, easily agreed upon the two prayer concerns: revival of the church and awakening of the lost. It spread quickly. By any measurement, it was united prayer and fasting that moved God to bring The First Great Awakening.

Within just a few years of Edwards' death in 1764, the spiritual state of the church again declined. Dr. J. Edwin Orr, eminent revival historian, described the conditions of our country at that time in these words:

> There was an unprecedented moral slump following the American Revolution (1775-1783). Drunkenness was epidemic. Out of a population of 5 million, 300,000 were confirmed drunkards. Profanity was of the most shocking kind. For the first time in the history of the American settlement, women were afraid to go out at night. Bank robberies were a daily occurrence. A poll at Harvard discovered not one believer in the student body. The great church historian Dr. Kenneth Scott Latourette wrote of this period: "It seemed that Christianity was about to be ushered out of the affairs of men." The Chief Justice of the Supreme Court, John Marshall, a concerned believer, wrote to a friend this assessment: "The Church is too far gone to ever be redeemed." (Mary Stewart Relfe, *Cure of All Ills*, p. 26)

Once again, God stirred the heart of a pastor, Issac Backus, to realize the necessity of united prayer. As Edwards before him, he wrote a paper entitled "A Plea for the Revival of Religion." It was distributed to pastors of every denomination in the United States, pleading for each man to set aside the first Monday of each month to open his church all day and conduct extraordinary prayer for revival. Almost every denomination joined in a call to their member churches, imploring them to unite in prayer and fasting. Congregationalists, Baptists, Presbyterians, Methodists, and independents came together in their local churches and prayed. Then they prayed together in their cities or area, crossing denominational barriers and beseeching God to bring desperately needed revival.

The answer to this united prayer and fasting became known as The Second Great Awakening (1794-1840). God did amazing things in response to the unified prayer and fasting of His people. Millions were converted and added to the church. The frontier of America had a particularly strong visitation from God through camp meetings, which not only caused the church to grow, but gave a new stability to life on the frontier.

Public education, the missionary movement, and the roots of the abolition of slavery came as a result of this revival and awakening. More than 600 colleges were started by different revivalists. The church began to be a great influence on society once again because it returned with passion to the Savior and lived in obedience to His call.

These situations illustrate that historically, believers have viewed their time as hopeless. They found that when they started to pray and fast, God heard and brought revival to the church and awakening to the lost.

Our day, too, is dark. There may never have been a darker time for the church of Jesus Christ in America than the times in which we find ourselves living. But there is hope. As Dr. Orr was fond of saying, "Whenever God is about to do something new with His people, He always sets them to praying."

David Barrett, leading demographer of the world Christian movement today, has given the following statistics from his extensive research:

1. Worldwide, there are about 170 million Christians committed to praying every day for revival and spiritual awakening.
2. Of these, 20 million believe that praying for revival and awakening is their primary calling in ministry within the body of Christ.
3. There are at least 10 million prayer groups seeking God for a coming world revival.
4. There are an estimated 1,300 prayer mobilization networks seeking to stir up the church to accelerated prayer for world revival and mission. (David Bryant, "God Is Up to Something," *Pray!*, Issue 1)

David Bryant responds to the above data in his book, *The Hope at Hand*:

If we know historically, as Dr. Orr suggests, this ground swell of prayer is a gift from God; if it is biblically accurate to teach that God has not only ordained the end but the means (the end being world revival, the means being the prayers of his people); if this massive chorus of prayer is increasingly focused on nothing less than national and world revival; and if, when God stirs us up to this type of praying, He does so because He is actually ready to answer us — *how can we believe otherwise than that world revival is bearing down on top of us?* (p. 31, emphasis added)

Passionate, persistent and convinced prayer is the key to revival. Prayer is not changing the heart of God, for His heart is already clear. He wants to bring revival and awakening. Prayer is presenting to God His own promises and petitioning these promises that they may be fulfilled by faith. "Prayer, then, is essentially laying before God His own promises" (W. Vernon Highan, *The Turn of the Tide*, p. 32).

Oswald Smith explains it this way in his tract *Effective Prayer*:

A promise by God is a pledge by God. It provides the warrant and forms the basis of the prayer of faith. The stability of a promise rests upon the character and resources of the One who makes it, even as the value of a check depends upon the honesty and resources of the one who signs it. The character and fidelity of God vouch for the credibility of the promises He makes. With God, promise and performance are inseparable. But promises must be distinguished from facts. We accept a stated fact of God's Word, but we plead a promise. When God proclaims a fact, faith accepts and acts upon it. When God makes a promise, we comply with its conditions, claim its fulfillment, and receive the promised favor. The function of the prayer of faith is to turn God's promises into facts of experience. The patriarchs through faith obtained the fulfillment of God's promises (Hebrews 11:33) and turned them into personal experience. The prayer of faith has its basis in neither outward circumstances nor inward feelings. It is when sight brings no helpful vision and comfortable emotions are largely absent that the prayer of faith finds its greatest opportunity. It springs from the naked promise or affirmation of the Word of God, for faith proceeds only from a divine warrant. The prayer of faith is the power which converts promise into performance.

Breaking Down Denominationalism

The second ingredient that is part of every revival and awakening is a breaking down of the walls of denominationalism. While there is nothing wrong with denominations, the sectarian spirit precluding Christians from having anything to do with the rest of the body of Christ is quite destructive. In The First Great Awakening, The Second Great Awakening, The Prayer Revival of 1857-59, The Welsh Revival of 1904-05, and The Azusa Street Revival of 1906-09, the kingdom of Christ was more important than the kingdom of denomination.

Iain Murray remarks:

> One mark of an outpouring of the Spirit of God is the presence of a stronger catholicity of spirit among believers. Only when churches put adherence to Christ first, can the world begin to recognize the real identity of those who bear His name. (*Revival and Revivalism*, p. 88)

In our day, we are witnessing intentional breaking down of the walls of denominationalism and racism that have divided and disfigured the body of Christ. Across this land, Christians are realizing the sin of racism that has divided us from one another and ruined our testimony to the lost world. The Spirit of God is eradicating the sin of white racial superiority in the Anglo church. In the churches of color, the sin of wrong response to persecution and exclusion is surfacing. God is doing something momentous. Across this country, pastors are meeting to fast and pray together. Groups of churches are meeting to fast and pray, crossing denominational and racial barriers. They are pleading with God to send a revival to His church, and to bring awakening to the lost. God is stirring up biblical unity (John 17) in our land.

Perhaps you have heard the story of the American man on a flight to England. As the plane was preparing to land, he looked out of the window and saw all of the stone fences in geometric design in the English countryside. A few months later, he flew over the same area he had seen before, but there were no fences. Puzzled, he asked the flight attendant what had happened to the fences. "O sir, you see, it's harvest time. The fences are still there, it's just that the harvest covers them up."

That's what always happens in revival. The fences of racial and denominational division are still there, but now the eyes of the church are on the harvest, not the fences.

Will this growing chorus of prayer and fasting that is crossing denominational and racial barriers move our heavenly Father to send the desired and needed revival and awakening? How can we believe otherwise?

A Thirst for God

One last ingredient must be present before God sends revival and awakening: an unquenchable thirst for God.

> The inevitable and constant preliminary to revival has always been a thirst for God, a thirst, a living thirst for a knowledge of the living God, and a longing and a burning desire to see Him acting, manifesting Himself and His power, rising, and scattering His enemies. The thirst for God and the longing for the exhibition of His glory are the essential preliminaries to revival. (Martyn Lloyd-Jones, *Revival*)

When a deep thirst for God causes us to unite in prayer and fasting and the barriers of race and sectarianism begin to fall, it is a sign of hope that corporate revival is closer than it has ever been.

Is revival near? I am asked that question regularly. As a result, I have come to understand that I may never see the revival for which I am praying and laboring. However, Zech. 9:12 has become a soft pillow for my heart: "Return to your fortress, O prisoners of hope." God is the author of revival. He will bring it when He chooses. But, it is coming! Make no mistake about it. My response, and I might add your response, is to be a man, woman, or young person of faith. We are, if you will, to be "prisoners of hope." Revival is closer then it has ever been.

QUESTIONS FOR REFLECTION

1. Do you agree that "we can't bring revival but we can prepare for it"? Why or why not?
2. What do you make of this quotation taken from the chapter: "The prayer of faith is the power which converts promise into performance." How does this tie in with revival and awakening?
3. How do you assess the present preparation of the church in the United States for revival and awakening? How do you assess the church you attend? How would you assess your own preparation?
4. Do you sense revival is near or far from the church? Why or why not?

CHAPTER FIVE

What Happens When Revival Comes?

In 1904, God used a young Welsh coal miner named Evan Roberts to usher in one of the most far-reaching revivals in world history. Thugh only 26, Roberts was a man of fervent prayer and radiant joy. A personal Pentecost began when God led him to agonize in prayer over the state of the church and his own soul. As the burden intensified, he began praying a simple prayer: "Bend me."

Roberts requested permission to speak one evening to a small group of 17 people at Moriah Chapel in Loughor. The next night Roberts spoke at a nearby missions chapel and the ice over people's hearts had begun to melt. Pastor Joseph Jenkins asked for testimonies. A young girl named Florrie Evans, who had been a believer only a few days, rose and with a trembling voice said simply, "I love Jesus with all my heart."

By week's end, after preaching each night, some 60 young people had surrendered their hearts to the Lord. Within 12 days of his first speaking engagement more than 800 people were crammed into the small chapel and homes had to be opened for prayer meetings. Then this passion to surrender spread to neighboring communities.

The presence of the Lord began to be felt in nearby Aberdare. Soon there was an explosion of God's presence over another 12 cities throughout Wales. By Christmas in 1904, the small Celtic country of Wales was in the middle of one of the greatest moves of God in the 20th century.

Roberts was a major proponent of singing and worshiping God in His presence. As congregations all over Wales worshiped the Lord, souls repented at hearing the gospel and were saved.

Jails in mining communities throughout the country were emptied, leaving police without much to do. Shops did little business because people were focused on revival. Businessmen still made money, though, because people were so convicted of sin they were paying old and forgotten debts, insisting that interest be included.

The Welsh revival and awakening began in November 1904 and only lasted until the summer of 1905. But in that short period, as many as 152,000 people came to a saving relationship with Jesus Christ.

The 1904 Welsh Revival is one of the best-documented and most well known revivals of all, and certainly one of the most powerful. Over a period of two years, the fire of the Holy Spirit swept over the whole principality, and was carried by visiting pastors to Norway, Japan, America, India, South Africa, and Korea, where further revivals broke out.

Sudden Coming

When revival comes, it is sudden. Even though the church is praying and believing that God will send revival, often it is caught by surprise. In the Acts 12 account of Peter's deliverance from prison, Christians were joined together in prayer for his release. The answer to their prayers stood at the door. Their response: "Peter kept on knocking, and when they opened the door and saw him, they were *astonished*" (v. 16, emphasis added).

All accounts of historical and present-day church revivals have this common denominator: Churches are surprised because revival comes so suddenly.

In reading of the revival that came to his church in January 1995, Pastor John Avant of Brownwood, Texas, journaled the following:

Our early service began as normal, about 8:30 a.m. with the auditorium about half full. When I offered the invitation, Chris Robeson, a student leader on campus, came forward and asked if he could speak. Ordinarily, I would have told him to talk to me after the service, but God led me to allow him to speak. Chris stood at the pulpit and read Joel 2:12: "Turn to Me with all your heart, with fasting, with weeping, and with mourning"

(NKJV). He began to weep and cry out to the Lord. He shared his desperate burden that the time had come for revival. People began to stream down the aisles. People started coming to the microphone spontaneously sharing Scripture and sharing their hearts. (Avant, McDow, and Reid, *Revival,* pp. 11-12)

Pastor Avant had taught on revival, and the church had been praying for revival, but when it came, it surprised them. Revival catches the believer unaware, in fear and astonishment. "Revival," Winkey Pratney reminds us, "is God springing a surprise on His creation" (*Revival: Its Principles and Personalities,* p. 21).

Along with the suddenness, there is a great conviction of sin brought about, most often through the preaching of the Word. This conviction grips both the believer and nonbeliever at the same time. During the season of revival the Spirit of God uses the sermons of His pastors to cause an incredible response among both the saved and unsaved in the church:

> There was nothing, humanly speaking, to account for what happened. Quite suddenly, upon one and another came an overwhelming sense of the reality and awfulness of His presence and of eternal things. Life, death and eternity seemed suddenly laid bare. (Joseph Kemp of Charlotte Chapel in Edinburgh, 1905)

Often in the midst of revival, a sinner, without any preparation or forethought, will suddenly be seized with an overwhelming conviction of sin. Sometimes this results in great agony of spirit. Charles Finney, a revivalist during The Second Great Awakening, said this about a meeting he held:

> An awful solemnity seemed to settle upon the people; the congregation began to fall from their seats in every direction and cry for mercy. If I had a sword in each hand I could not have cut them down as fast as they fell. I was obliged to stop preaching. (Pratney, p. 24)

Asa Nettleton, also a revivalist in The Second Great Awakening, said much the same:

> Did you ever witness two hundred sinners with one accord in

one place weeping? The scene is beyond description . . . I felt as though I was standing on the verge of the eternal world; while the floor under my feet was shaken by the trembling of anxious souls in view of the judgment to come. (Pratney, p. 24)

Recently, I was leading a meeting of more than 700 pastors when suddenly one of the men, under great conviction of God, cried out. It really was more of a loud wail, continuing for some time. He was so convicted by the seriousness and gravity of his sin that all he could do was wail and moan. When he finally stopped, he confessed his sin, repented, and the men around him prayed for him.

Revivals appear to come suddenly, especially to the individual, though God's preparation for a people may require years. We saw that in the revival that came under Andrew Murray's ministry. His father and intercessors had prayed for more than 30 years. Murray himself had prayed for some time. Yet when revival came, he tried to stop it because he didn't know what it was.

Corporate revival is both a point in time as well as an ongoing process and experience in the life of the church. Usually God uses powerfully anointed preaching to bring great conviction to the sinner, which then leads to repentance. Richard Owen Roberts describes repentance like this:

First and foremost, repentance is not any single thought or act. Repentance is not something once done and forever accomplished. Repentance is an ongoing process. One must be forever repentant. It is not enough to have once felt sorrow over sin. No single change of mind will suffice. No individual act of self abasement will meet the biblical requirement. True repentance affects the whole person, alters the entire lifestyle and does not cease. (*Revival*, p. 66)

True repentance is a day-by-day, week-by-week, month-by-month, year-by-year process. It is living a broken life before the great God of the universe who searches our hearts. (See Appendix B for the process of repentance.)

Unusual Manifestations

Sometimes unusual things transpire in revival. Manifestations may occur that can be difficult to understand and different from our normal experiences with God. This is the part of revival that causes the most controversy, both inside the church with Christians, and outside the church.

Mendell Taylor's description of the Cane Ridge Revival that occurred in Kentucky in 1801 provides a picture of manifestations that occurred in a revival. (It is important to remember that every revival is different. This description should not be taken as a proof of what *will* occur.)

> At the Cane Ridge Revival in Bourbon County in 1801, 20,000 people arrived for a six-day camp meeting. The noise was like the roar of Niagara. The vast sea of human beings seemed to be moved upon as if by a storm. Some of the people were singing, others praying, some crying for mercy in the most piteous accents, while others were shouting most vociferously. My heart beat tumultuously, my knees trembled, my lips quivered, and I felt as though I must fall to the ground. A strong supernatural power pervaded the entire mass of people. The scene was indescribable. At one time I saw at least five hundred swept down in a moment as if a battery of a thousand guns had opened upon them and then immediately following, shrieks and shouts that rent the very heavens. (Joy Dawson, *Pray!*, Issue 4, p. 27)

Revival is never "business as usual" in a church. In fact, if all of the revivals in church history were studied, the overwhelming number of them might be described as "messy." At a minimum, revival usually disturbs the order and length of the service. Numerous pastors who have experienced some form of revival all testify that the scheduled order of worship is abandoned. What would happen if the service at your church lasted four hours because God's presence was manifested and no one wanted to leave? Think about the poor nursery staff!

In revival history, some or all of the following manifestations have been present:

- An agony of spirit, which manifests itself in great tears, sorrow, and often loud wailing.
- An overwhelming sense of God's holiness, which leads to what may appear to be depression. This sometimes lasts for days before forgiveness is understood and experienced.

- An almost indescribable joy, which relates to other manifestations.
- Falling to the ground in a trancelike state.
- A violent shaking coming over an individual causing his/her body to tremble.
- Falling to the ground and rolling (thus, the term "holy roller").

Do physical manifestations *have* to accompany a revival? The best answer from the Bible (see Acts 2:1-13) and church history seems to be that there will always be some manifestations of the Spirit of God accompanying revival. The key is not to assume that you can predict what God is going to do in the revival. We must not become consumed with an interest in, or a dependence on, certain manifestations to authenticate revival. Satan often uses fascination with those events to sidetrack and ultimately kill a revival of the Spirit of God in people's lives or in a church.

During the camp meetings (like the Cane Ridge Revival) of The Second Great Awakening (1794-1830), many unusual and loud manifestations were experienced. Indeed, those people would have assumed that a revival could not have occurred apart from the manifestations they had experienced. Yet at the very same time, in the New England states, revival was happening with the same kind of powerful results but with very different experiences.

The Rev. John B. Preston of Rupert, Vermont, wrote:

> Our prayer meetings were crowded, and solemn to an amazing degree. No emotions more violent than shedding of tears, and no appearance of wildness and disorder occurred. Nothing appeared but a silent, fixed attention, and profound solemnity, the most resembling my idea of the day of judgment of any scene I ever witnessed. Infidelity retired, or was overcome by the bright manifestations of divine power and grace. (Murray, *Revival and Revivalism*, pp. 138-139)

The manifestations that God used there in New England were silence and tears. It is important to note that God is the author of revival and He will send the manifestation(s) that He chooses. It is the responsibility of the leadership of a church to pastor a revival and to prohibit any manifestations from detracting from God's agenda.

One pastor put it this way: "We monitor and pastor the revival." (That is, certain manifestations are controlled or not allowed.) "If something is not of the Lord or drawing attention away from the work of the Spirit, the ushers will move the individual outside the building. We don't allow people to distract" (*Enrichment Journal*, Winter 1997).

Manifestations are never to become the focus or a substitute for experiencing God. However, we must keep the following words of Jonathan Edwards in the forefront of our thinking as we await the coming revival:

> That a revival is always a disfigured work of God, and the more powerful the revival, the more scandalizing disfigurement we may expect to see. A work of God without stumbling blocks is never to be expected. (J.I. Packer, *Jonathan Edwards and the Theology of Revival,* as quoted in Robert Bakke's *The Concert of Prayer,* p. 50)

In other words, don't despair if there are abuses or mistakes made—in fact, there very well may be. Where mistakes are made, purposely or unknowingly, repent quickly and learn from the sin, but don't allow that to quench the Holy Spirit's work of revival.

Satan, the master counterfeiter, attempts to keep step with the work of God by distracting us and causing us to desire a manifestation of God rather then the very person of God.

> Satan will keep his grip on men as long as he can. But when he can do that no longer, he often tries to drive them to extremes. Satan wants them to dishonor God, and wound the Christian faith in that way. (Jonathan Edwards, *Do It Again Lord*, Archie Parrish, ed.)

Pastor and lay leaders, you may need to monitor the revival as it comes to your church. But don't squelch it! Laymen, pray for the leadership of your church, that they will have the wisdom and discernment of God to pastor well the heaven-sent revival.

Study the subject of revival with others in your church so that when these kinds of situations occur in your midst, you will not be caught unprepared or bound up with fear. A good place to start is with *An Urgent Appeal* (see Appendex C: Bibliography). Understand

and be convinced that it is not manifestations that authenticate a true revival. It is the changed lives and conversions that prove the validity of a revival and awakening.

<hr>

QUESTIONS FOR REFLECTION

1. Why does the suddenness of corporate revival cause difficulties?
2. How do you feel about manifestations in corporate revival? Does this cause you concern? Why or why not?
3. What would be your response if next Sunday during your worship service, there was a sudden move of God? How do you think others in your church would respond? What could/should you do to help your church prepare for revival?

CHAPTER SIX

What Are the Effects of a Revival?

As we read in the last chapter, though short-lived, the revival in Wales (1904-1905) had a worldwide effect. One example of this continuing revival occurred in 1908 in Northern China. Missionary Jonathan Goforth recounted the change that transpired in the city of Taiyuan because of this revival:

It was wonderful how mightily the Spirit of God worked in the church of Taiyuan during these days. So marked was His presence, indeed, that it was quite a common thing to overhear people in the city telling each other that a "new Jesus" had come. Their reason for saying this was that for years many of the professing Christians had been cheating their neighbors and quarrelling with them. Some, indeed, had gone so far as to revile their parents and beat their wives. It seemed that the other Jesus was too old or had lost His power to keep them in order. But this "new Jesus," it appeared, was doing wonderful things. He was making all those old backsliders get up before the whole church and confess their sins, and afterwards go right back to their heathen neighbors and pay back anything that they owed, and beg forgiveness of all whom they had wronged. But what was the greatest surprise of all was that they should even go so far as to abase themselves before their wives, asking their pardon for the way in which they had mistreated them. In this way a revival served to carry conviction to the great mass of people outside the church, that the Living God had come among His people." (Jonathan Goforth, *By My Spirit*, Bethany Publishers)

Another effect of the Welsh revival was felt in the United States. The following headline from the *Denver Post,* dated January 20, 1905, caught some of the change happening in the church. This revival of the church was obviously getting the attention of those who were not Christian. The headline read:

"ENTIRE CITY PAUSES FOR PRAYER EVEN AT THE HIGH TIDE OF BUSINESS AS THE SOUL RISES ABOVE SORDID THOUGHTS!"

The article began: "All Denver was held in a spell under the influence of the power that is not of ourselves, that makes for righteousness. The Spirit of the Almighty pervaded every nook. The thousands of men and women radiated the Spirit which filled them, and the clear Colorado sunshine was made brighter by the reflective glow of the light of God shining from happy faces. Seldom has such a remarkable sight been witnessed—an entire great city in the midst of a busy weekday, bowing before the throne of heaven and asking the blessing of the king of the universe."

How Will We Know?

Those are exciting testimonies of revival. We wonder: *Can that happen in our church, in our community?* How will we know if we have revival? What are some effects that result when revival comes?

The first effect of revival happens to the saint. To see the primary effect of revival, one must look to the church. Revival awakens the church from sleep: "The hour has come for you to wake up from your slumber, because our salvation is nearer now than when we first believed" (Ro. 13:11). In revival, the believer is radically changed by the manifest presence of God. Holiness suddenly becomes the driving force of the believer's study and lifestyle. Everything is viewed in the light of what God wants.

Sin is exposed and confessed, often publicly. Relationships that were broken are healed. Debts that were ignored are paid. A deep burden for those without Christ stirs in the heart. The saint now shares the gospel freely and unashamedly with all in his sphere of influence. A new song manifests in the heart and on the lips. People begin singing as they work, go to school, and walk the streets. Great joy is a hallmark of revival. In other words, a new man, a new woman, a new young person appears, and people stand in awe of what God has accomplished. Saints become lights in a dark world. This is the difference between renewal and corporate revival and awakening. In renewal the effect on the person or congregation remains inside the walls of the church. But when corporate revival occurs it spills out of the church, the lost come to Christ, and there can be a great effect on the society. Revival always has an effect inside and outside of the church.

The next effect is on the sinner. In a true revival, many who are separated from God come to a saving faith. This usually begins within the church itself, as those who have "a form of godliness" actually become partakers of the wonderful saving grace of Jesus Christ.

When a true revival occurs, very quickly within a town, city, or region, scores of unsaved come to the cross of Christ. For example, in The Great Prayer Revival of 1857-58, on September 23, 1857, Jeremiah Lanphier started a prayer meeting from 12:00 p.m. to 1:00 p.m. for business people. It met at the Old Dutch Church on Fulton Street in New York City. The first week, six came. The next week, 20 showed up. Within six months, 10,000 businessmen out of a population of 800,000 were gathered for prayer. By January 1858, there were at least 20 other prayer meetings occurring throughout New York City. Almost simultaneously, noon prayer meetings arose across America. Among the daily prayer meetings reported: 150 towns in Massachusetts, 200 in New York, 60 in New Jersey, 65 in Pennsylvania, 200 in Ohio, 150 in Indiana, 150 in Illinois, 50 in Missouri, and 60 in Iowa.

Suddenly revival and awakening broke out. It is estimated that at the high tide of the revival, 50,000 people a week were converted. The number of people who joined the churches in the two years of the revival averaged 10,000 a week (Relfe, *The Cure of All Ills*, p. 62). One student of prayer and revival has estimated that if a revival of like magnitude were to come to the United States today, it would result in the salvation of roughly 18 million people.

The third effect of revival is on society. As a result of either new-found faith or revival of faith that had lost its zeal, suddenly saints begin to view their responsibility to society in a new light.

Jonathan Edwards, writing in 1746, said that a full-fledged revival will involve a balance between personal concern for individuals and social concerns. He stated further that religious meetings, prayer, singing, and religious talk will not promote or sustain revival in the absence of works of love and mercy, which will "bring the God of love down from heaven to earth" (*Jonathan Edwards: A Treatise Concerning Religious Affections,* as quoted by Relfe, p. 23).

During The Second Great Awakening, there was a linkage between personal holiness and social conscience. One writer has said that in The Great Prayer Revival of 1857-1858, the theme "immediate personal holiness and social righteousness" became as significant to that move of God as "justification by faith" was to the Reformation (Relfe, p. 45).

The church of Jesus Christ has a great opportunity today. Because of the changes the government has made in the welfare system, and a host of other societal ills, the church has the privilege to step into the void and minister in the name of Jesus. But this will not happen in great numbers until revival comes because Christians are too preoccupied with themselves. As a result, believers largely don't feel compelled to serve others. However, when God manifests His presence and reveals our sin to us, and revival comes, then Christians will move into the society with broken hearts and genuine compassion with a motivation to serve. When this occurs the impact will be so great on those who do not believe that millions will be swept into the kingdom of God. As a result, our society will be radically altered.

When God brings revival to the church, followed by an awakening of the lost, the inevitable result is that society is changed, because suddenly there are more Christians than nonChristians. This has been true in every major revival in history. Revived and awakened people change societies.

Earlier, we noted that the condition of our society reflects the condition of the church. The reverse is also true. When the church of Jesus becomes what Christ died to make us and an awakening of the lost follows that revival, it is inevitable that the society of which we are a part will be changed as a result (Mt. 5:13-16).

This was evident in both biblical as well as church history revivals. Therefore, we should expect nothing less to occur in our nation if God should so choose to bless the American church with revival and awakening.

CHAPTER SEVEN

What Dangers Are Inherent in Revival?

Fulton Street in New York City is said by most people to be the beginning of the "Prayer Meeting Revival"—started by businessman Jeremiah Lanphier—that eventually swept down from the northeastern states all the across the country. As many as 1 million people came to Christ within a year's time. But African-American slaves in the south were already seeking God for revival and encountering the Lord's manifest presence months before Lanphier's first prayer meeting. The first rumblings of revival actually began in Charleston, South Carolina, in the middle of 1857 at Anson Street Presbyterian Church.

Pastored by Dr. John Lafayette Girardeau, Anson Street Presbyterian Church had 48 black members and 12 white members. In 1857, the church began a series of prayer meetings, seeking God and petitioning Him to send a spiritual awakening. They sought, inquired of the Lord, and sought some more. Dr. Girardeau had made a decision not to preach until the Spirit of the Lord had made Himself known. So the prayer meetings continued and the congregation of believers, most of whom were slaves, continued to patiently seek and wait for the Spirit to make Himself known.

And then it happened: One evening while seeking the Lord in prayer, Girardeau felt as if a surge of electricity struck his head and went through his entire body. He began to sing a hymn of worship. Following the hymn he softly stated: "The Holy Spirit has come.

Preaching begins tomorrow evening." He then dismissed the church.

But no one left. Looking around the sanctuary, Girardeau saw that the Lord's presence had also rested upon his congregation. They were worshiping, praying, and weeping for their unbelieving loved ones and friends. By the time he was able to redismiss the congregation, it was after midnight.

Word of this encounter got out. Every night for the next eight weeks, Girardeau preached to crowds of more than 2,000. The presence of the Lord had descended on the city. Thousands of Charlestonians, both black and white, were saved during the ensuing months! Congregations of all denominations throughout the city had members added to their number daily!

Girardeau was to eventually make a name for himself by participating in theological debates over issues of public worship and as a leader in his denomination's hierarchy, but he never again experienced the move of the Spirit in such a large measure. His life will best be remembered for those few days when at the age of 30, along with the heart of a few African-American slaves, he gave everything he had to find the manifest presence God and spiritually trigger one of the greatest moves of the Spirit of God in American history.

We all long to see a move of God's Spirit like the one that descended on Charleston in the late 1850s. But many of us are also cautious when it comes to seeking moves of God like this. Why? Because it is beyond our known experience. We need not be afraid of a move of God, but we are right to keep some level of caution when it comes to supernatural moves. A reading of revival history will quickly show that there are dangers inherent in revival. And we need to be aware of them.

When we see an apparent move of God's Spirit, there are both some questions we can ask and some attitudes we can avoid.

Is It from God?

First, we must always ask if the revival is from God. Satan always tries to undermine the work of God. He counterfeits the things of God so that we are seduced into either accepting that which is false or doubting that which is from God.

Jonathan Edwards played a pivotal role in The First Great Awakening in 1732. After observing the revival and awakening taking place in his church and city, he wrote what many consider to be one of the great pieces of revival literature, *The Distinguishing Marks of a Work of the Spirit of God*. In it, he offered criteria, based on 1 John 4, for determining whether a movement was a work of God. In summary, Edwards believed these characteristics would be present if it was a true revival:

- Love for Jesus is increased.
- The Holy Spirit operates against the interests of Satan's kingdom.
- Love for, and obedience to the Scriptures increases.
- People are led to truth.
- People are led to a greater love for God and man.

Thus for Edwards, revival is both a doctrinal corrective and a practical experience, changing the way one lives.

Do We Judge Others by Our Experience?

Another danger in revival is the judging of others by our experience. The thinking is, "If others have not experienced everything exactly as I have, then what they are claiming as revival cannot possibly be an authentic move of the Spirit of God." Unfortunately, in the history of revival, this often happens. We must be careful not to expect a replica experience of revival and awakening.

This happened in the Welsh Revival. One of the sad side effects of this great move of God was the ensuing attitude of those who had been saved during the revival. Many did not recognize the salvation of their children as being legitimate because they had not been saved during a time of revival. Sadly, within a generation, the church in Wales was as cold as it had ever been largely because these misguided people judged others by their own experience.

Satan often derails corporate revival through this method. Those who have experienced the extraordinary presence of God become filled with pride. This is especially true of young believers. They begin to think that "the secret" of the Lord has been revealed exclusively to them. Edwards recalled many instances in which "the Devil has come in at this door after some eminent experience and extraordinary communion with God, and has woefully deluded and led them astray" (Ian Shaw, *Young People in the Great Awakening*).

Refusing to Believe a Move Is from God

Many will not believe that what is happening is a move of God. These people can be wonderful, well-meaning, mature believers. How could this happen you might ask? There are two reasons. First, what they see happening doesn't fit their model of what they believe a revival should be. Maybe many years prior, they had experienced a move of God's Spirit in their church. But what is happening today doesn't look exactly like that move of God. So they assume this move cannot be from God. Second, they refuse to believe because it is led by those who they consider to be the wrong people. Maybe it started with the youth group, or with a new believer. *Surely,* they think, *a real move of God would begin with the pastor or the elders; not someone as immature as this person.* Perhaps this is the reason Andrew Murray at first tried to stop the revival he was so diligently praying for. It didn't start with the pastor, through powerful preaching.

When apparent moves of God come, we need to watch, pray, and discern. Revivals often are derailed or hindered by believers who preach and write against anything that they either didn't start or that is outside of their formula for revival. "Friendly fire" is to be expected. As we study revivals of the past, and then read the sermons and articles by Christians opposing them, we are amazed. Either these opponents were arrogant, or they were unprepared for revival. It is vitally important that you distinguish and discern true revival. However, be careful not to force revival to align with your formula, for it may not.

Scripture warns us not to "blasphem[e] against the Holy Spirit" (Mt. 12:31). A trap for many Christians is to attribute to Satan anything with which they are not personally familiar. But many of these rejected moves might be a work of God. This rejection of the work of the Spirit is a rejection of Christ. Be careful!

Fear of Losing Control

Fear is another danger. Revival brings with it a sense that one is not in control. And we humans hate to lose control! Pastor Joseph Kemp said this regarding The Welsh Revival (1904-1905): "To the curious, the meetings appear disorderly; but to those who are in them and of them, there is order in the midst of disorder. The confusion never gets confused; the meetings are held by invisible hands" (Relfe, *Cure of All Ills,* p. 145).

In describing what one of the meetings was like in that same revival in Wales, G. Campbell Morgan said, "It was a wonderful night, utterly without order, yet characterized from first to last by the order-liness of the Spirit of God" (Relfe, p. 146).

For those who feel they must maintain control, revival can be frightening. It is the primary reason why many want nothing to do with revival at all. Any time there is an interruption in the orderly flow of a service, the first emotion we often experience is fear. Turning to Jesus at this time can bring calm and direction.

When you begin to experience revival in your church, you should immediately pray for great discernment and sensitivity to lead in this special move of God's Spirit: "Revival activities, beliefs, and behaviors must be spiritually discerned through the written Word of God and biblical principles, not by our emotions, opinions, religious back-grounds or personal likes or dislikes. We are to test the work of the Spirit by the principles in the Word of God" (Frank Damazio, *Seasons of Revival,* p. 141).

Other Dangers

Another danger in revival is to give man the glory that belongs only to God. When revival starts happening in a church, we are often prone to look at the leader. We think there is something special or unique in him or her that brought this about. God tells us, "I will not give my glory to another" (Is. 42:8). The purpose of revival is to draw all men to the Savior. Revival is all about the Lord Jesus Christ.

Often in revival, man attempts to duplicate by human effort what God has done somewhere else. We fall victim to a pragmatic formula—if it worked over there, it will work in our church as well. The key to revival and awakening is waiting on God and asking Him to do for us what we are unable to do for ourselves. We must plead with Him, implore Him, and storm heaven in the name of Jesus, asking the Father to send the revival; but, we must never in our own strength try to manipulate or force revival. Our own efforts will fail.

Revivals are sometimes short-lived because of hasty decisions to move individuals into leadership positions. We must be careful not to place new believers or recently revived believers in a place of leader-ship too soon. Because God has done such an amazing transforma-tion in someone's life, we equate that with spiritual maturity. It is not. Scripture is very clear that placing a new believer in any leadership position might cause them to fall into sin (1 Tim. 3:6).

One last danger that should be mentioned is associated with public confession and repentance. The leadership of the church should develop guidelines for their congregation regarding the practice of confession, because most often revival brings public sharing of sin. We must not allow someone to sin in the midst of his or her confession. An example would be giving too much detail about a sexual sin, or mentioning someone by name who sinned with them. To keep this from happening it has been suggested that godly men and women be appointed by the leadership of the church, to whom the confession is first given, prior to being shared with the entire congregation. They then determine the propriety or impropriety of allowing the confession to be made before the congregation. If a confession is deemed inappropriate for the entire congregation, it may be wise to have a small group of godly men and women to whom the sinner can confess, in this way honoring Scripture, while protecting the congregation. (For further insight, see, *Repentance* by Richard Owen Roberts.) This matter is something that can be taught prior to the revival and undoubtedly during the revival itself. (For further study, see the pamphlet *Council on Open Confession* by Jim Elliff.)

Conclusion

As we have seen in this chapter, there are a lot of potential dangers in revival. But remember, the biggest danger is not letting the Spirit of God move. While we must be aware of the dangers, we should never let our discomfort with the unexpected cause us to automatically deny revival.

QUESTIONS FOR REFLECTION

1. Does the issue of corporate revival scare you at all? Why? Why not?
2. Make a list of the dangers mentioned in the chapter.
3. Which dangers, mentioned in the chapter, are you most susceptible to and why?
4. Which dangers, mentioned in the chapter, might your church be susceptible to? Why? What can you do to assist your church to overcome this danger?

CHAPTER EIGHT

What Can You Do to Prepare for Revival?

Described by some as the most powerful revival in Baptist history, the Shantung (China) Revival (1927-1937) was birthed in a time of military conflict, social instability, and lukewarmness in the church. The quest for revival began with a small group of Southern Baptist missionaries and was carried forward by a Norwegian Evangelical Lutheran named Marie Monsen—a small woman who had overcome, by perseverance and the power of the Holy Spirit, the formidable task of learning the Chinese language, as well as numerous bouts with illness, spiritual dryness, and depression.

The revival began as intercessory concern for the Chinese Christians who were left behind in China's inland by discouraged missionaries. This led to the stark realization that the missionaries themselves were in great need of a fresh touch from on high. As the Southern Baptist missionaries devoted themselves to prayer, their burden for awakening grew. Starting with one hour of prayer early in the morning, they eventually were praying till noon. Like Jacob and the angel at the river Jabbok, they would not let go until God blessed them.

In 1930, the North China Mission (an organization of Southern Baptist missionaries) meeting reported on the status of the mission field. According to C. L. Culpepper, author of *Spiritual Awakening: The Shantung Revival* and a witness to the events, three Chinese evangelists made discouraging reports of work among "dead" churches. A note of despair and spiritual hunger permeated their messages. Another missionary reminded the group that in the North China Mission at least 70 churches had "died." Many, she felt, had accepted God's grace as an outside coating but had only "covered" their sins, not received forgiveness. A well-known Chinese evangelist, in despair over the seeming hopelessness of the work, told the group that more than 1,000 people had been converted to Christianity, not to Christ.

A nominal faith that possessed the form of religion, but not the power, characterized Chinese converts at the time. The missionary leaders began to realize that if the promise of God's blessing did not resonate deeply in their own hearts, revival would not freely flow out to the people.

While a hunger for the presence of God began to permeate the lives of the missionaries, revival would not have been complete without the prophetic declaration of God's Word. Late in 1930, Marie Monsen declared, "A great revival is coming soon, and it will begin in the North China Mission." When questioned on this, she responded, "Because God has a covenant with His people. It is as true today as it was when He made it. He said, 'If my people, which are called by my name, shall humble themselves, and pray, and seek my face, and turn from their wicked ways; then will I hear from heaven, and will forgive their sins, and will heal their land'" (2 Chron. 7:14, KJV). She added, "I believe God is going to send a revival to you and your people because you have fulfilled those four conditions."

Monsen began to speak on the serious nature of sin, the necessity of the new birth, sensitivity to sin in one's own life, a quest for a life of holiness, prayer for revival in China, renewed faith in God's Word, and reconciliation and restitution among the believers. The strength of her proclamations did not lie so much in her oratorical skills as they did in her simple faith in God. In the words of Mary Crawford, an American missionary, "Miss Monsen herself is one of the quietest speakers I ever heard. There was very poor singing, no invitation for public decisions, only the quiet question, 'Have you been born again?'" Quoting from one missionary's letter: "Everything otherwise has been so quiet. Were it not for a wonderful spirit of prayer and an occasional testimony, no unknowing visitor would believe we were in the midst of a revival."

As the revival spread, the missionaries heard about a woman who had been healed after 28 years of paralysis, and they set off on rented bicycles to her village 20 miles away to learn more. The woman's pastor related the story to them. The church had planned a revival meeting but did not consider the option of praying for the sick. Mrs. Chiao (the paralyzed woman), however, believed that if the church would pray for her, she would be healed. Lacking faith themselves, the pastor and the congregation were finally convinced, brought her to the church, and placed her in front of the communion table. Here they fervently prayed for her, and in a few minutes they heard a noise. They looked up to find Mrs. Chiao walking up and down the church aisle!

Subsequently, this little church of 50 members began to be blessed by God, and they systematically evangelized not only their own village, but the surrounding ones as well. Not long after, it was estimated that there was at least one Christian in each of the 1,000 homes in the town.

Revival prayer meetings sprang up not only in churches, but also in schools, hospitals, and seminaries. Students in one school, many without a saving faith in Christ, came under the convicting power of the Holy Spirit. They began weeping for their sins and confessing sins of cheating, stealing, lying, and disobedience to parents. Their repentance lasted deep into the night. As a result of this marvelous move of God, the principal announced that the school would be closed to allow the revival free course. Services were held every day, morning and evening, and people filled the aisles and came forward to pray, tears of repentance staining the wooden floor. By the end of 10 days, 600 girls and 900 boys were saved (Martin Chow, "A Humble Cry, *Pray!*, Issue 22).

What Can We Do?

While the church cannot birth revival, God does use means to prepare the way for revival. This chapter will focus on the means, or things that we can do, that will help prepare the way for a revival of Christ's church, and consequently, an awakening of the lost.

Believe Revival Is Biblical

First, you must resolve that revival is indeed something that God desires and that it is biblical. Revival and awakening must be a conviction. Until this issue is settled, you will not be able to pray powerfully or enthusiastically for revival, nor will you be able to join with believers in activities designed to foster revival. Without this conviction, you will hold back from wholehearted support. If you do not believe revival is important, you will never prepare for it.

Live a Life of Brokenness

Second, the Bible calls us to live a life of brokenness. *Brokenness, The Forgotten Factor of Prayer* by Mickey Bonner, suggests a prayer that a Christian needs to pray every day: "Lord, reveal me to me as You see me." As soon as we pray that, we are brought to the place of brokenness. We realize how far we have fallen from God's standard, and we relinquish the belief that we have arrived. Rather, with a "broken and contrite" (the word literally means to be crushed) heart, we turn to God. As we do this, we discover that God not only hears us but also allows us to live in a revived state: "I live in a high and holy place, but also with him who is contrite and lowly in spirit, to *revive* the spirit of the lowly and to revive the heart of the contrite" (Is. 57:15, emphasis added). Revival is found only in the life of a person, a church, a community, and a nation that understands and lives in brokenness. (For a comparison of pride and brokenness, which God has used to bring revival to thousands, see Appendix A.)

Pray

A third thing we can do to help prepare for revival is pray. When the people of God individually and corporately "storm the gates of heaven" in response to the prompting of God, then revival is imminent.

Revival often follows extraordinary prayer as God's people are moved to pray in a whole new way. Suddenly there is fervency—an intensity that takes over their prayer life in imploring God to bring revival. The length of their praying is increased. All-night prayer meetings become common. Often the prayer becomes very emotional, including crying out and a literal aching for God to bring revival to their sick church. There is a sense of confidence that what we are praying is going to come to pass because it is God's will. There is a sense of "seeing" the revival before it comes. One writer has said,

> When prayers and strong pleas for revival are made to God both day and night, when the children of God find they can no longer tolerate the absence of revival blessing, when extraordinary seeking of an extraordinary outpouring becomes extraordinarily earnest, and when the burden of prayer for revival becomes almost unbearable, then let praying hearts take courage for the Spirit of God who is the Spirit of revival has brought His people to this place for His purpose. (Richard Owen Roberts, *Revival,* p. 60)

This "prayer preparation" needs to be in place so that once the revival and awakening comes, sustained intercessory warfare praying will continue for the newly revived and converted, as well as for the revival itself. The whole issue of deliverance prayer will also need to have been taught, because of the satanic bondage with which many of the newly revived and converted have been oppressed.

You might consider augmenting your prayer for revival with fasting. Worldwide, millions of Christians have committed to regular prayer and fasting. Many are beginning their fast after dinner Thursday and skipping breakfast and lunch on Friday to pray that God would send the needed revival. Others participate in an initiative called "First Friday Prayer." Here, individuals and churches cry out to God for revival on the first Friday of each month. First Friday prayer themes are available in each issue of *Pray!* magazine or by going to www.ifapray.org.

One of the moves of God in our day that is assisting revival preparation is the blending of worship with prayer. Indeed, this "harp and bowl" (see Rev. 5:8) approach to intimacy with God is helping to create a climate that encourages worshipers to long for, and cry out to God for His manifest presence.

Become Familiar with Revival

A fourth thing that you can do to prepare the way for revival is to read and become familiar with the subject. As you read what God did in the revivals of the past, it will give you a confidence of what He might do in our day. In the back of this book is a list of resources to assist you. Remember, the purpose of this book is to take you to a deeper understanding of, and a greater hunger for, revival. Don't stop now.

Additionally, if you are convinced that God is going to send a revival and awakening, you should alert your church to what is coming. Most churches in America are not prepared to disciple newly revived believers or new converts. Consider this: Would your church be able to disciple 100 newly revived believers or converts immediately? Most churches wouldn't be ready because they don't have a discipleship program in place or leaders trained. If the revival and awakening began tomorrow, millions of spiritual babies might die for lack of spiritual nurturing. If we are convinced that revival and awakening is coming, we should start now to train ourselves, and the people of our church, so that when God releases the revival and awakening, not one of the revived and awakened is lost. But suppose the revival and awakening doesn't happen, what then? You would be left with a church of discipled believers. Is that a bad thing? It almost sounds biblical doesn't it?

Lastly, we need to be messengers of the coming revival. If we have a conviction in our spirit that revival and awakening in the church of America is God's desire, then we must begin addressing it and preparing for it.

Questions for Reflection

1. Do you have deep conviction that revival and awakening is the desperate need of the church in America? If yes, why? If not, why?
2. What, if anything, are the next steps that you need to take in preparing for revival?
3. Is the church you attend prepared for a coming revival and awakening? If yes, what has the church done to come to this place of preparedness? If no, what is it that you can do to help your church prepare?

CHAPTER NINE

Increase Your Longing and Hope

Lord, I tearfully ask: Teach me to pray with groanings so that there are earthquakes in hell. Teach me the groanings of the Spirit until angels stand in awe. Teach me Spirit-born intercession that changes history. Teach me the birth pangs of the Holy Ghost until hell-shaking revival is born. Lead me into travail that will hold back divine judgment from the nations for a little season. Let me be a living sacrifice on the altar of prayer, "bleeding to bless," until flood tides of mercy sweep the nations. Lord, break my heart in intercession until my eyes, like those of Jeremiah, are a fountain of tears weeping for the slain of an educated, but spiritually dead people. (Leonard Ravenhill, *Revival God's Way*)

Oh Breath of Life, come sweeping through us,
Revive Thy Church with life and pow'r;
O Breath of Life, come cleanse, renew us,
And fit Thy Church to meet this hour.
(Bessie Porter Head)

Abba Father, we are like the rebellious children of Isaiah's time. We, Your church, do not want to listen to Your instructions. We are rebellious children, unwilling to listen and to receive Your message for repentance. . . . We do not want to be confronted

with Your truths. We reject Your messages; instead we rely on
false teaching of other gods, we live in oppression and fraud and
with plans to reject Your teachings. You have been calling us to
repentance, but we do not want to have anything to do with it.
You long to be gracious and compassionate to Your saints and
You are calling us to come back into covenant relationship with
Jesus Christ. You are the God of justice, giving blessing to those
who depend on You. So through intercessory prayer O God, I
ask for forgiveness and plead for revival. . . . Pour out Your Spirit
in these last days O Lord, and revive Your church! O Lord speak
powerfully to Your church exposing everything that is false, las-
civious, and full of greed. O God of compassion, please exercise
that compassion and send a mighty Holy Ghost revival to my
church and this nation. (David Wilkerson, *David Wilkerson
Newsletter*)

Lord, I give myself to You, whatever the cost may be. Take every
aspect of my life and use me for Your kingdom to glorify Your
name. I'm not here on earth to do my own thing, to seek my
own fulfillment or my own glory. I'm not here to indulge my
desires, to increase my possessions, to impress people, to be
popular, to prove I'm somebody important, or to promote
myself. I'm not here even to be relevant or successful by human
standards. I'm here to please You. To live like this, I yield myself
to You, to know You, to worship You, to obey You, and to grow
in Your Holy Fear. I'll do anything that You want me to do, go
anywhere You want me to go, and say anything that You want
me to say. Father, there isn't any gift that You have for me that I
don't want. If You want to use me in a way that I'm not used to,
I yield myself to that. Today I affirm my love for You, my God,
and I choose to live and minister in Your way. I trust You Lord
to do that which I cannot do for myself. Teach me, guide me,
empower me to fear Your name. In Jesus' name, Amen. (*Portions*
authored by Myers, Jacobs, Schlafer)

Holiness Zones

During the revivals and awakenings God has brought to this country,
the impact in many geographic areas has been unusual. Often, God

brought a special sense of His presence to a region. As a person approached a city, they could literally feel the presence of God there. Imagine then, whole areas of America so saturated with God, that you could literally sense God's presence. During The Second Great Awakening (1794-1830), a divine influence seemed to pervade Utica and Rome, New York, during a season of revival. People would feel compelled to get right with God the moment they entered the city limits. So strong was this presence of God, that the term "zone of holiness" was coined to describe what was transpiring there.

During The Prayer Revival of 1857-1859, the Holy Spirit seemed to hang like a cloud over much of the East Coast. At times, the cloud seemed to extend out into the ocean. The following was reported by such a large and diverse number of people that the accounts cannot be doubted.

> Those on ships approaching the East Coast at times felt a solemn, holy influence even hundreds of miles from land. Revival began on one ship before it reached the coast. People on board began to feel the presence of God and a sense of their own sinfulness. The Holy Spirit convicted them and they began to pray. As the ship neared the harbor, the captain signaled, 'Send a minister.' Another commercial ship arrived in port with the captain, and every member of the crew converted in the last 150 miles of the journey. Ship after ship arrived in the ports of the East Coast with the same story: Passengers and crew were suddenly convicted of their sin and turned to Christ before they reached the American coast. (Wesley Duewel, *Revival Fire,* pp. 133-134)

Charles Finney said,

> Many times great numbers of persons in a community will be clothed with this power, when the very atmosphere of the whole place seems to be charged with the life of God. Strangers coming into it and passing through the place will be instantly smitten with conviction of sin and in many instances converted to Christ. (Arthur Wallis, *In The Day of Thy Power*)

These stories about the "zones of holiness" end this study in order to cast a vision for your prayer life. Wouldn't it be something if the "hell holes" of our inner cities and suburbs could become zones of holiness? Wouldn't it be something if America became a clean, vibrant, holy place? We cannot make it happen, but our God can! He has done it before! Would you join with me in asking . . . begging . . . imploring . . . pleading with our heavenly Father to bring a revival and awakening to our church and then to our land?

If a revival and awakening is to come, you and I must be changed. Nancy Leigh DeMoss has said, "Revival is not just another emphasis to add to our already overcrowded agendas. It's not an option. It's not just a nice idea. A meeting with God in genuine revival is our only hope; our church's only hope; our nation's only hope."

I couldn't agree more. If a genuine revival and awakening doesn't come very soon, then we will move from the remedial judgments of God that we have been experiencing to a more severe judgment.

Someone once asked the British evangelist, Gypsy Smith, "How do you start a revival?" Smith replied, "If you want to start a revival, go home and get a piece of chalk. Go into your closet and draw a circle on the floor. Kneel down in the middle of the circle and ask God to start a revival inside the chalk mark. When He has answered your prayer, the revival has begun" (Tom Phillips, *Revival Signs*).

A couple of years ago, a group of us were praying for revival and awakening when suddenly one of the men broke into tears and sobbing. This lasted for some period of time. When he finally stopped crying, he started to sing an old hymn. Here's what he sang:

Pass me not O gentle Savior, hear my humble cry;
While on others thou art calling, do not pass me by.
Savior, Savior, hear my humble cry;
While on others thou art calling, do not pass me by.

What's the point of this book? *You are the revival that God is seeking!* Don't allow Him to pass you by today; rather, like Jacob in the Bible, hang on to Him. Don't allow Him to leave you until you are changed. Join with others from your church to pray for a revival and awakening there. Join with others in your city to pray for the revival of Christ's church and the awakening of the lost. Join with people of different races, cultures, and church traditions. In united prayer, ask God to bring revival and awakening to your church, your city, then to America, and finally . . . to the world.

Restore us again, O God our Savior, and put away your displeasure toward us. Will you be angry with us forever? Will you prolong your anger through all generations? Will you not revive us again, that your people may rejoice in you? Show us your unfailing love, O LORD, and grant us your salvation. (Ps. 85:4-7)

Appendix A: Proud Spirits and Humble Hearts

Nancy Leigh DeMoss contrasts characteristics of proud, unbroken people who are resistant to the call of God on their lives with the qualities of broken, humble people who have experienced God's revival. Read each item on the list and ask God to reveal which characteristics of a proud spirit He finds in your life. Confess these to Him. Ask Him to restore the corresponding quality of a broken, humble spirit in you.

Proud, Unbroken People	**Broken People**
Focus on the failures of others	Overwhelmed with a sense of their own spiritual need
Self-righteous; have a critical, fault-finding spirit; look at own life/faults through a telescope but others' with a microscope	Compassionate; forgiving; look for best in others
Look down on others	Esteem all others better than self
Independent/self-sufficient spirit	Dependent spirit; recognize need of others
Maintain control; must be my way	Surrender control
Have to prove that they are right	Willing to yield the right to be right
Claim rights	Yield rights
Demanding spirit	Giving spirit
Desire to be served	Motivated to serve others
Desire for self-advancement	Desire to promote others

Driven to be recognized and appreciated	Sense of unworthiness; thrilled to be used at all; eager for others to get the credit
Wounded when others are promoted and they are overlooked	Rejoice when others are lifted up
"The ministry is privileged to have me!"	"I don't deserve to serve in this ministry!"
Think of what they can do for God	Know that they have nothing to offer God
Feel confident in how much they know	Humbled by how much they have to learn
Self-conscious	Not concerned with self at all
Keep people at arm's length	Risk getting close to others; willing to take the risks of loving intimately
Quick to blame others	Accept personal responsibility and can see where they are wrong
Unapproachable	Easy to be entreated
Defensive when criticized	Receive criticism with a humble, open heart
Concerned with being "respectable"	Concerned with being real
Concerned about what others think	All that matters is what God knows
Work to maintain image/protect reputation	Die to own reputation

Find it difficult to share their spiritual needs with others

Willing to be open and transparent with others

Want to be sure no one finds out about their sin

Willing to be exposed (once broken, they don't care who knows)

Have a hard time saying, "I was wrong. Would you forgive me?"

Quick to admit failure and to seek forgiveness

When confessing sin, deal in generalities

Deal in specifics

Concerned about the consequences of their sins

Grieved over the cause/root of their sin

Remorseful over their sin— got caught/found out

Repentant over sin (forsake it)

When there is a misunderstanding, wait for the other to come and ask for forgiveness first

Take the initiative to reconcile conflict; see if they can get to the cross first

Compare themselves with others and feel deserving of honor

Compare themselves to the holiness of God and feel desperate need for mercy

Don't think they have anything to repent of

Continual heart attitude of repentance

Don't think they need revival (think everybody else does)

Continually sense their need for a fresh encounter with the filling of the Holy Spirit

Appendix B: The Gift and Process of Repentance

"The goodness of God leads you to repentance." (Ro. 2:4, NKJV)

REVELATION is what happens when you are reading the Bible, listening to a sermon, talking with a friend, reading a book, or listening to God, and you suddenly grasp a truth of God that you had not understood previously.

RECOGNITION is when you realize that this truth is describing you or your situation.

REMORSE/GODLY SORROW is being sorry that you failed your heavenly Father in this regard. That leads to confessing it as sin and asking God's forgiveness. This is often where most Christians stop. But to truly repent we must do more than confess.

RESOLUTION is choosing the mind of Christ: "I need a new mindset, a new way to think—I need to think like Jesus." The word used most often in the New Testament for repentance is the Greek word *metanoia*: *meta* = change; *noia* = mind. Thus, in repenting of sin, you choose the mind of Christ, and as a result, your thinking, emotions, and will begin to be conformed to His. Some refer to this as the act of your will that goes in an opposite direction from your now recognized and confessed sin.

REVOLUTION/REFORMATION occurs as your mind, emotions, and will begin to change. As Christ's mind becomes your way of thinking and living, you become more and more like Christ. Everything about you starts to change. There is a revolution and reformation in your life and the way you live.

RESTITUTION/RESTORATION is what you do when you see the effect your sin has had on others. You ask their forgiveness, and if necessary, and/or possible, you make restitution for your sin.

REGULAR/RAPID is a lifetime practice. You immediately repent when the Spirit of God reveals your sin. Rapid, immediate obedience becomes your attitude. It is never enough to say, "I repented." Rather you must say, " I am repentant." It is not a one-time experience, but a lifetime attitude and practice.

Appendix C: Bibliography — A Reading List on Revival

Armstrong, John. *True Revival.* Eugene, OR: Harvest House, 2001.

Avant, John, Malcolm McDow, and Alvin Reid. *Revival: The Story of Current Awakening in Brownwood, Ft. Worth, Wheaton, and Beyond.* Nashville, TN: Broadman & Holman Publishers, 1996. Quotes used by permission.

Bakke, Robert O. *The Power of Extraordinary Prayer.* Wheaton, IL: Crossway Books, 2000.

Blackaby, Henry T., Grant Adkisson, and Richard Owen Roberts. *Foundations of Revival, Volume One.* Hendersonville, NC: Lighthouse Productions, 1993. Quotes used by permission.

Blackaby, Henry T., and Claude V. King. *Fresh Encounter: God's Pattern for Revival and Spiritual Awakening.* Nashville, TN: Life Way Press, 1993. Quotes and diagram used by permission.

Bonner, Mickey. *Brokenness, The Forgotten Factor of Prayer.* Houston: Mickey Bonner Evangelistic Association, 1995.

Brown, Michael. *Revolution.* Ventura, CA: Regal Books, 2000.

Bryant, David. *The Hope at Hand.* Grand Rapids, MI: Chosen Books, Inc., a division of Baker Book House Company, 1995. Quotes used by permission.

Burns, James. *The Laws of Revival.* Edited by Tom Phillips. Wheaton, IL: World Wide Publications, in cooperation with the Institute of Evangelism, Billy Graham Center, 1993.

Coleman, Robert. *The Coming World Revival.* Wheaton: IL: Good News Publishers/Crossway Books, 1995. Quotes used by permission.

Damazio, Frank. *Seasons of Revival.* Portland, OR: BT Publishing, 1996.

DeMoss, Nancy Leigh. *Brokenness: The Heart God Revives.* Chicago: Moody Press, 2002.

Duewel, Wesley. *Revival Fire.* Grand Rapids, MI: Zondervan Publishing House, 1995. Quotes used by permission.

Edwards, Brian H. *Revival.* County Durham, Great Britain: Evangelical Press, 1990.

Edwards, Jonathan. *The Distinguishing Marks of a Work of the Spirit of God.* See *The Spirit of Revival* by Archie Parrish for a modernized text.

Elliff, Jim. "Counsel of Open Confession" (pamphlet). Kansas City, MO: Christian Communicators Worldwide.

Engle, Lou. *Digging the Wells of Revival.* Shippensburg, PA: Destiny Press, 1998.

Finney, Charles. *Lectures on Revival.* Grand Rapids, MI: Fleming H. Revell, a division of Baker Book House Company.

Gillies, John. *Historical Collections of Accounts of Revival.* Carlisle, PA: Banner of Truth, 1991.

Higham, W. Vernon. *The Turn of the Tide.* Wheaton, IL: International Awakening Press, 1996. Quotes used by permission.

Kaiser, Walter Jr. *Revive Us Again.* Nashville, TN: Broadman & Holman Publishers, 1999.

Lloyd-Jones, Martyn. *Revival.* Wheaton, IL: Good News Publishers/Crossway Books, 1987. Quotes used by permission.

Murray, Iain H. *Revival and Revivalism: The Making and Marring of American Evangelicalism, 1750-1858.* Carlisle, PA: The Banner of Truth Trust 1994. Quotes used by permission.

National Revival Network. *An Urgent Appeal.* Colorado Springs, CO: NavPress, 2003.

Ortlund, Raymond Jr. *When God Comes To Church.* Grand Rapids, MI: Baker Books, 2000.

Parish, Archie. *The Spirit of Revival: Discovering the Wisdom of Jonathan Edwards.* Wheaton, IL: Crossway Books, 2000.

Phillips, Tom. *Revival Signs: Join the New Spiritual Awakening.* Gresham, OR: Vision House Publishing, Inc., 1995.

Pratney, Winkie. *Revival: Its Principles and Personalities.* Lafayette, LA: Huntington House Publishers, 1994.

Ravenhill, Leonard. *Why Revival Tarries.* Minneapolis, MN: Bethany Fellowship, 1959.

Relfe, Mary Stewart, Ph.D. *Cure of All Ills.* Montgomery, AL: League of Prayer, Inc., 1988. Quotes used by permission.

Roberts, Richard Owen. *Revival.* 1993. Wheaton, IL: Richard Owen Roberts Publishers 1993. Quotes used by permission.

Shaw, Ian. *Young People in the Great Awakening.* Carlisle, PA: The Banner of Truth Trust.

Tyre, Jacquie. *Ready for Revival: A 40-Day Heart Journey Toward the Fullness of Christ.* Colorado Springs, CO: NavPress, 2002.

Wallis, Arthur. *In the Day of Thy Power: The Spiritual Principles of Revival.* London: Christian Literature Crusade, 1956.

Winslow, Octavius. *Personal Declension and Revival of Religion in the Soul.* Carlisle, PA: The Banner of Truth Trust, 1993.

Multiple Copy Discount

Use in Small Group or Sunday School Class!

REVIVAL 101

UNDERSTANDING HOW CHRIST IGNITES HIS CHURCH
By Dale Schlafer

Revival 101 will encourage and challenge your congregation. Why not buy multiple copies for use in small groups, Sunday school classes, or to stimulate discussion among church leaders.

QUANTITY	DISCOUNTS*
2 – 24 copies..........$6.40 ea (20% off)*	
25 – 99 copies........$5.60 ea (30% off)*	
100+ copies ....$4.80 ea (40% off)*	

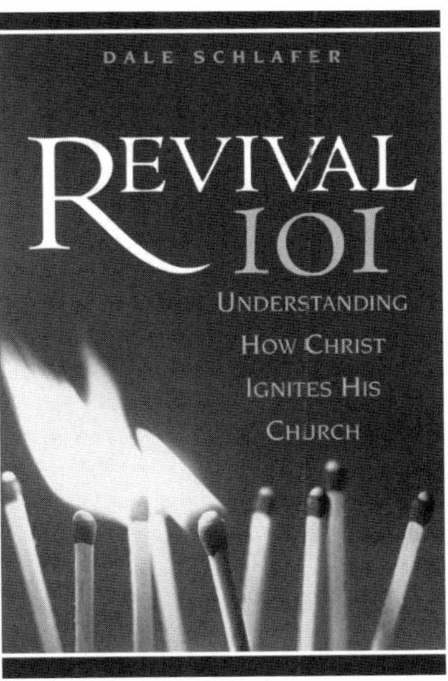

1-57683-442-5 $8*

To order call 1-800-366-7788 (or 719-548-9222)

7am-5pm M-F, MST

Or visit our website: www.praymag.com

*plus shipping/handling and applicable sales tax   Offer #6387